WE COME FROM

France

TERESA FISHER

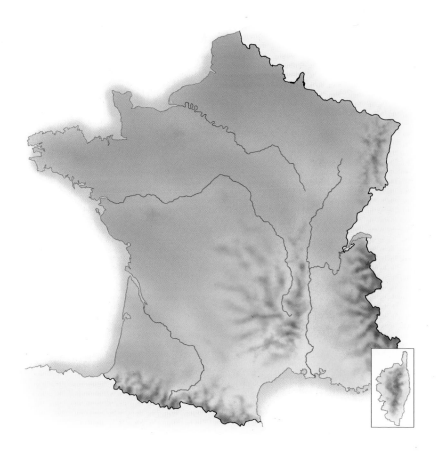

HODDER
Wayland

an imprint of Hodder Children's Books

WE COME FROM

Brazil • China • France
Germany • India • Jamaica • Japan
Kenya • Nigeria • South Africa

Most of the people you are about to meet live in a town in France called Toulouse. Like any country, France has many different types of lifestyles. People live in the countryside as well as in towns and cities.

Cover: Pierre and his friends have some fun on their bicycles at the side of the Garonne River.

Title page (from top to bottom): Shoppers search for bargains at the flea market in Toulouse; wild goats graze in the Pyrénées; people relax outside a café in Aix-en-Provence; a master chocolate maker shows his chocolate clowns; and a woman buys some fish from an indoor food market.

Contents page: A woman looks for shellfish on the beach.

Index: The Batiste family set off on a bicycle ride.

All Hodder Wayland books encourage children to read and help them improve their literacy.

 The contents page, page numbers, headings and index help locate specific pieces of information.

 The glossary reinforces alphabetic knowledge and extends vocabulary.

 The further information section suggests other books dealing with the same subject.

Series editor: Katie Orchard
Designer: Jean Wheeler
Production controller: Tracy Fewtrell

Picture Acknowledgements: All the photographs in this book were taken by Dorian Shaw. The map artwork on page 5 was produced by Peter Bull.

First published in 1999 by Wayland (Publishers) Limited Reprinted in 2001 by Hodder Wayland, an imprint of Hodder Children's Books

© Hodder Wayland 1999

British Library Cataloguing in Publication Data
Fisher, Teresa
  We come from France
  1. France – Geography – Juvenile literature
  2. France – Social conditions – 1945– – Juvenile literature
  I. Title II. France
  944' .0839

ISBN 0 7502 3817 8

Typeset by Jean Wheeler, England
Printed and bound by G. Canale & C. S.p.A., Turin

Contents

Introduction

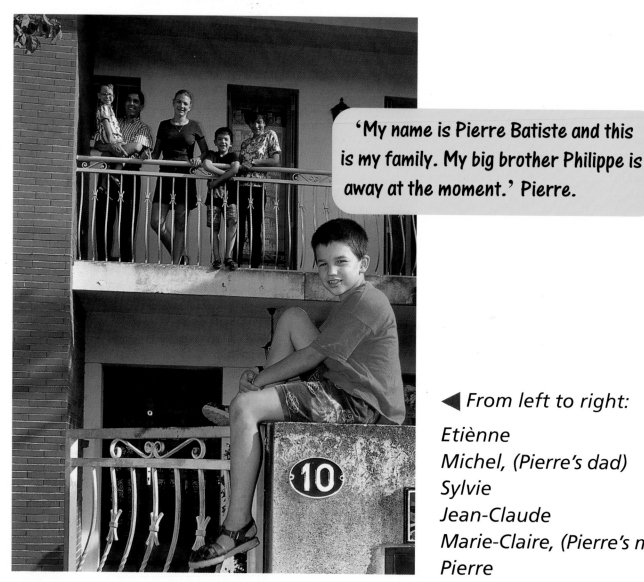

'My name is Pierre Batiste and this is my family. My big brother Philippe is away at the moment.' Pierre.

◀ *From left to right:*

Etiènne
Michel, (Pierre's dad)
Sylvie
Jean-Claude
Marie-Claire, (Pierre's mum)
Pierre

Pierre is nine years old. He lives in Toulouse
with his parents, his three brothers, Etiènne,
Jean-Claude and Philippe, and his sister, Sylvie.
Toulouse is a large town in southern France.
You can see where it is on the map on page five.

▶ *France's place in the world.*

▼ *This book takes you to Toulouse as well as the rest of France.*

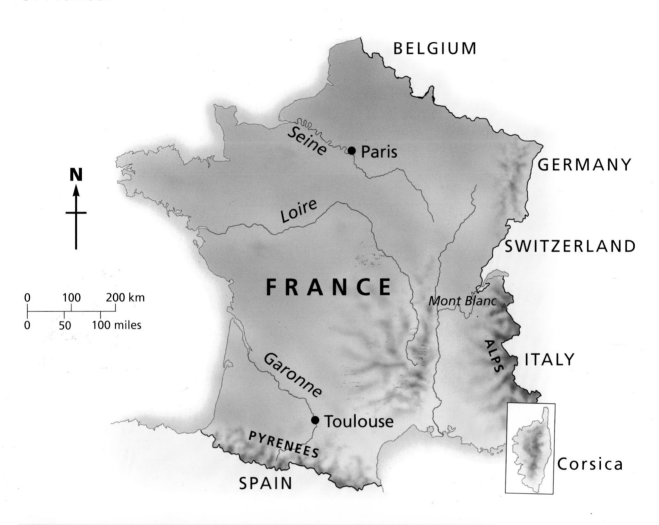

FRANCE

Capital city:	Paris
Land area:	551,670 square kilometres
Population:	58 million people
Main language:	French
Main religion:	Roman Catholicism

The Land and Weather

France is the largest country in western Europe. It is bordered by Spain, Germany, Switzerland, Luxembourg and Belgium.

Most large cities in France are near its coast or along a river.

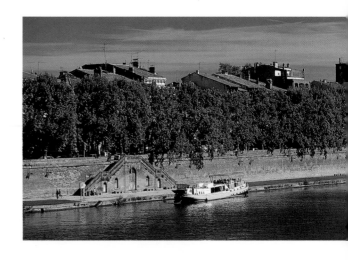

▼ *Many French people spend their holidays in France.*

▲ *The city of Toulouse lies on the Garonne River.*

In the south of France, the summers are long, warm and dry, and the winters are mild and rainy. The weather is cooler and wetter in the north.

▲ *During winter, snow covers the Pyrénées Mountains.*

▲ *There are many pig farms near Toulouse.*

France has more farmland than any other country in Europe. The main crops are wheat, barley, grapes and apples. Dairy farmers make tasty cheeses and pig farmers produce lots of different types of sausages.

'I use this tool to check that my goat's cheese is ready to eat.' Jean-Luc, cheesemaker.

Around Toulouse, where Pierre lives, there are hills, woodland and meadows. To the south are the high mountains of the Pyrénées. To the south-east there are the sandy beaches of the Mediterranean.

▼ *French apples are sold all over the world.*

Home Life

Most people in France live in large towns and cities where the homes are mainly apartments. They don't usually have gardens, but often have balconies where the family can sit or hang the washing.

In the suburbs, just outside the cities, some people live in houses or bungalows.

▲ Many people in France live in apartments like these.

◄ In villages, some people live in old stone cottages and farmhouses.

► This woman has planted lots of flowers on her balcony.

11

Pierre's family live in a house in the suburbs of Toulouse. It has a large living room, kitchen, bathroom, four bedrooms and a sunny balcony. Pierre shares a bedroom with his brother Philippe.

'Sharing a room is fine. My brother is usually out, so I can have friends to visit.' Pierre.

◀ *Pierre often helps his mum around the house.*

Pierre's family spends a lot of time together. At weekends, they often visit friends or go cycling in the countryside.

In the evenings, the children often stay up late, reading, watching television or chatting to their parents over dinner.

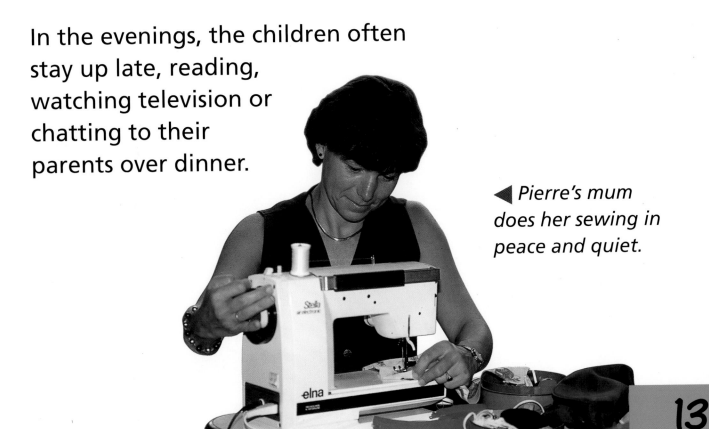

◀ *Pierre's mum does her sewing in peace and quiet.*

13

Food and Cooking

French people love their food and wine. France is well known for its delicious cooking, using fresh food from colourful local markets.

▶ *French people often like to relax outside cafés.*

'My customers know that everything on my stall is fresh. That's why they keep coming back!' Mr Dupont, greengrocer.

14

ALÉES | CRÊPES SUCRÉES

SUCRE
CONFITURE
CHOCOLAT
BEURRE
RHUM
GRAND MARNIER

◀ *Delicious hot pancakes, called* crêpes, *are a favourite snack.*

One typical French dish is snails, served hot with garlic butter. *Crêpes* and pâté are popular foods. France is famous for mushrooms called truffles. Pigs are used to sniff them out. Truffles are expensive and are only eaten on special occasions.

The Batiste family always starts the day with breakfast. Usually they have a long, thin, crusty loaf of fresh bread called a baguette, with a bowl of coffee or hot chocolate.

▲ *Chocolate* éclairs *are filled with delicious cream.*

'For a treat we have croissants for breakfast at the weekend.' Pierre.

The main meal is usually dinner in the evening, when the whole family gets together. But on Sundays, they have a huge midday lunch with four or five courses, which sometimes lasts all afternoon.

▲ *Pierre and his family sit down to eat lunch together.*

17

Working Hard

France is well known for making aeroplanes, cars and trains. But it is even more famous for making goods, such as perfume, tasty cheeses, wine and bubbly champagne. These goods are sold all over the world.

▲ *A customer carefully chooses some perfume.*

▼ *There is a huge selection of cheeses in France.*

'I really like my job. It's nice to be able to work from home.' Pierre's dad.

Most people in Toulouse work in the banks, shops or companies in the city centre. Many people work in the big factories outside the city.

Pierre's dad works for an insurance company. He spends four days each week travelling to see customers, and one day working at home.

School

Lessons usually start at half-past-eight in the morning and end at half-past-four in the afternoon.

Most schools have a two-hour lunchbreak. Some children go home for lunch, while others have their lunch at school.

▼ *There's always a queue for the school computers.*

▲ *Pierre walks to school with his mum and friends.*

Pierre goes to elementary school near his home. It is a large school with more than 500 pupils. There are about 30 boys and girls in Pierre's class. Pierre's favorite class is computer studies.

▼ *This is Pierre's geography class.*

◀ The children sometimes spend their spare time in the school library.

On Wednesday afternoons, children can play sport or take part in fun activities such as painting, drama or dance at local youth clubs. Most schools have classes on Saturday mornings.

▶ These children are learning karate at a youth club.

'I normally do about one hour's homework every night before dinner.' Pierre.

Spare Time

The French love sport, especially football and cycling. Most French families spend their holidays in France, in the mountains or on the beaches.

In his spare time, Pierre has fun with his friends, watching television, going to the cinema, reading comics and playing lots of sports.

▲ *Surfing is a popular weekend sport.*

▶ *In-line skating is the latest craze in France.*

'I love playing computer games. My friend, Lucas, is always trying to beat my score.' Pierre.

Looking Ahead

'I love cycling. One day I want to ride in a bike race like the *Tour de France*.' Pierre.

France will always be famous for its food, fashion, industry and farming.

Now more and more visitors are coming to France, to see some of its attractions, such as its beaches, ski resorts and, of course, EuroDisney.

▶ The modern Cité de l'Espace *(Space City)* theme park in Toulouse is popular.

How to Play *Boules*

Boules is the national game of France. It can be played outside on any area of flat ground, with small groups of friends. These are the rules:

• Everyone stands behind a line.

• The first player throws a small wooden ball called a *cochonnet*, or 'piglet' a short distance.

• He or she then throws the first *boule* as close to the 'piglet' as possible.

▶ *Pierre's dad explains the rules.*

• The second player tries to throw his or her *boule* even closer to the 'piglet'.

• All the other players take it in turns to throw their *boules*. Sometimes they hit each other's *boules*. This makes the game even more exciting.

• The winner is the person whose *boule* is closest to the 'piglet' at the end.

◀ *Pierre tries to throw his boule as close as possible to the 'piglet' ball.*

France Fact File

Money Facts

▼ France's money is the Franc, which is divided into 100 centimes. £1 is about the same as 10 francs. If you look closely at a 50 franc note, you will see a picture of the Little Prince, from the famous book of the same name, written by a French writer called Antoine de Saint-Exupéry.

Famous People
Famous French people include Napoléon (an army general who became Emperor) and Charles Perrault who wrote *Sleeping Beauty* and *Cinderella*. Perhaps you have heard of them.

Stamps
▲ Most French stamps are red or blue with a picture of 'Marianne' on them. Marianne is not a real person. She is a symbol of the French Republic. Some stamps have pretty pictures or cartoons on them.

◄ The French Flag
The French flag or *Tri-colore* ('three-coloured') is red, white and blue. Red and blue represent the city of Paris and white is the traditional colour for French kings.

Mountain Facts
The highest mountain in France is Mont Blanc, in the Alps (4,807 metres).

River Facts
The longest rivers are the Loire, the Rhône, the Seine and the Garonne.

The Seine is 776 kilometres long. ►

The Fastest Trains in the World
French trains (called TGVs) are the fastest in the world, reaching speeds of up to 300 kilometres per hour.

Bastille Day
There are over 400 festivals in France. The biggest one is Bastille Day, on 14 July. This festival celebrates France becoming a Republic. This means being governed by a chosen president, not ruled by a king or queen.

Cheese Selection
◄ There are over 365 cheeses in France – a different one for every day of the year!

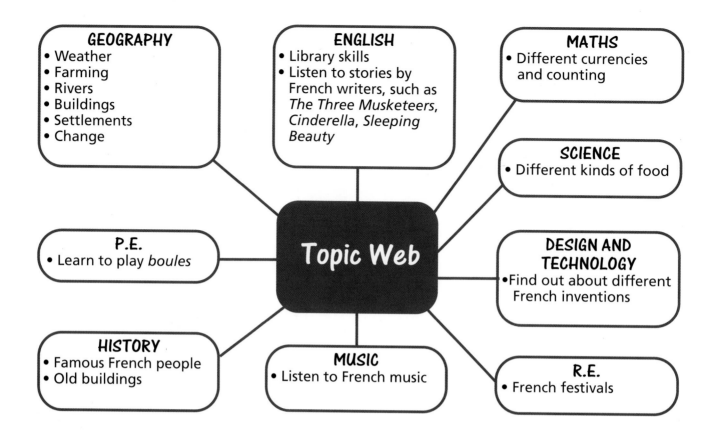

Extension Activities

GEOGRAPHY
- Do we eat any foods that come from France? Investigate packets and labels.
- How many different types of building can the children find in this book?

DESIGN AND TECHNOLOGY
- Find out about hot air balloons and the Montgolfier brothers.

ENGLISH
- Write a postcard to a friend describing what there is to see in Toulouse.
- Read the story of *The Little Prince*.

SCIENCE
- Make an easy French recipe, such as an omlette.

P.E.
- Make your own *boules* area.
- Make a board game of the Tour de France.

MUSIC
- Learn some simple French songs, such as Frère Jacques.
- Listen to the French National Anthem.

MATHS
- Make graphs or pie charts from the statistics in the fact boxes.

HISTORY
- Find out about Joan of Arc, Louis XIV (the Sun King) and Versailles.

Glossary

Balcony A platform outside a window, usually with railings.

Border The imaginary line dividing two countries.

Bungalow A house on one floor.

Flea market A street market where people can buy second-hand goods.

Latest craze The most popular thing at the moment.

Pâté A paste made from mashed and spiced meat.

Suburbs Areas of houses and shops at the edge of a town or city.

Tour de France A special bicycle race across France that takes place every year.

Traditional Something that has been done in a certain way for a very long time.

Further Information

Information Books
Country Topics - France by Anita Ganeri (Watts, 1993)
Picture a Country by Henry Pluckrose (Franklin Watts, 1998)
The Usborne First Book of France by Louisa Somerville (Usborne, 1993)

Fiction
Degas and the Little Dancer, A story of Edgar Degas by Laurence Anholt (Frances Lincoln, 1995)
The Little Prince by Antoine de St Exupéry

Music
Un, Deux, Trois: First French Rhymes selected by Opal Dunn. A collection of French nursery rhymes for young children. Includes an audio-cassette. (Frances Lincoln, 1996)

Useful Addresses
Maison de la France (French Government Tourist Office), 178 Piccadilly, London W1V 0AL. Tel: 0891 244123
France House, Digbith Street, Stow-on-the-Wold, Gloucestershire GL54 1BN. Tel: 01451 870871 for books, tapes, videos, posters and maps.

Index

All the numbers in **bold** refer to photographs.